Isabelle Pipahl

Arthur Miller's "The Crucible" and its relation to McCarthyism of the American 1950s

GRIN Publishing

Bibliographic information published by the German National Library:

The German National Library lists this publication in the National Bibliography; detailed bibliographic data are available on the Internet at http://dnb.dnb.de .

Imprint:

Copyright © 2008 GRIN Verlag GmbH
Print and binding: Books on Demand GmbH, Norderstedt Germany
ISBN: 978-3-656-89443-8

This book at GRIN:

http://www.grin.com/en/e-book/289170/arthur-miller-s-the-crucible-and-its-relation-to-mccarthyism-of-the-american

GRIN - Your knowledge has value

Since its foundation in 1998, GRIN has specialized in publishing academic texts by students, college teachers and other academics as e-book and printed book. The website www.grin.com is an ideal platform for presenting term papers, final papers, scientific essays, dissertations and specialist books.

Visit us on the internet:

http://www.grin.com/

http://www.facebook.com/grincom

http://www.twitter.com/grin_com

FACHARBEIT
im Leistungskurs Englisch

Arthur Miller's <u>The Crucible</u> and its relation to
McCarthyism of the American 1950s

Verfasserin: Isabelle Pipahl

Table of Contents

1. Introduction

Arthur Miller, one of the most important sociocritical dramatists of the 20th century, treats in his famous play <u>The Crucible</u> the witch hunts of Salem in 1692.

Considering this drama, the biography of Miller and the political situation in the date of origin of <u>The Crucible</u>, I would like to clarify the coherences between the drama and the highhanded persecution of inculpable humans in the American 1950s, at the time of McCarthyism.

The first part of my work deals with Arthur Miller, his life and his play <u>The Crucible</u>. In this part I would like to elucidate Miller's personal connection to the anti-communist campaign. Furthermore, I would like to show the destructiveness of rumours with regard to the executions happened in the late 17th century and accurate reflected in <u>The Crucible</u>. Moreover, I will enlarge upon the effects of the religion, in this case Puritanism, on the behaviour of the bourgeois and the justice.

The second part of my work deals with Joseph McCarthy, his life, the commencements of McCarthyism, the course of the trials and decline of McCarthyism. In this part I would like to show the arbitrariness of Joseph McCarthy with which he accused innocent people. Furthermore, I will enlarge on the cruelly effects of such persecutions, which destroy the person's futures and, as to <u>The Crucible</u>, the whole life.

Part three of my work will consist of conclusions about the impact of McCarthyism and Arthur Miller's drama <u>The Crucible</u>.

2. Arthur Miller's The Crucible

2.1 Biography

Arthur Asher Miller, who was born at October 17th in 1915 in New York as the son of a Jewish textile factory owner, has since the publication of Death of a Salesman been called "one of the century's three great American dramatists".[1] Arthur attended Public High School in Harlem from 1920 to 1928, ere he moved with his parents and siblings Joan and Kermit to Brooklyn in 1929.

After graduating from Abraham Lincoln High School in 1932, Arthur Miller attended Ann Arbor University of Michigan, to major Journalism, from 1934. During his academic studies, Arthur wrote his first play No Villian in 1936, and gained the Avery Hopwood Award in drama. After this success, Arthur Miller transferred to an English degree course. Since 1938 Miller worked for the Michigan Daily Newspaper ere he returned to New York. As from 1947 "Arthur Miller was firmly established as an American playwright".[2] Particularly his play All My Sons obtained the New York Drama Critics' Circle Award and the Donaldson Award. In 1949 the 33 – year – old Arthur Miller won the Pulitzer Prize and the New York Drama Critics' Circle Award for his play Death of a Salesman. Arthur Miller's drama The Crucible, "a drama of universal significance"[3], was premiered in 1953 and won the Antoinette Perry and the Donaldson Award.

In 1956 Arthur Miller "was subpoenaed to appear before the Un-American Activities Committee"[4], because he was implicated with communistic parties. Given that Arthur Miller denied an alliance with the communists and refused to declare names of communists known to him, Arthur Miller was sentenced to imprisonment.

From 1956 to 1960 Arthur Miller was wedded to Marilyn Monroe, for whom he wrote the screenplay The Misfits. After the matrimony with Marilyn Monroe, Miller married a third time. His wife was Inge Morath, an Austrian

---

[1] http://www.kennedy-center.org/calendar/index.cfm?fuseaction=showIndividual&entitY_id=3762&source_type=A
[2] http://www.kennedy-center.org/calendar/index.cfm?fuseaction=showIndividual&entitY_id=3762&source_type=A
[3] Corrigan, Robert W. "Arthur Miller A Collection of Critical Essays"; Ed. Warshow, Robert, "The Liberal Conscience in The Crucible"; Prentice-Hall: New Jersey, 1969. p.111
[4] Mahoney, John. "Guide to The Crucible", Charles Letts & CO. Ltd: London, 1988 p.5

photographer, with whom Arthur had two children. Altogether Arthur Miller had four children, two from his first marriage.

The last work published by Arthur Miller in 1987 was his autobiography Timebends: A life, "in which he recalls his childhood in Brooklyn, the political turmoil of the 1950's, and the later half of the century".[5]

Arthur Asher Miller died of heart failure at February 10th in 2005 at the age of 89 in Roxbury, Connecticut.

2.2 Summary

The story takes place in the puritan New England town Salem in Massachusetts.

Reverend Samuel Parris, the local minister of Salem, descries a group of young girls, among his daughter Betty, his niece Abigail Williams and a black slave named Tituba, dancing in the forest. Two of the girls, Betty Parris and Ruth Putnam, fall into a "coma-like state"[6] when they are at home. But when the diseases of Betty and Ruth cannot be healed, rumours of witchcraft and of a pact with the devil arise. However, Abigail Williams swears that the girls only danced in the forest and that they do not have anything to do with the devil or witchcraft.

Reverend Parris orders, for fear of his daughter, Reverend Hale, an expert of witchcraft, to help the girls. Initially Abigail does not want the other girls to admit anything, nobody could account for what they did in the forest, neither that they did not conjure spirits nor that Abigail drank blood. Not until Tituba confesses conjuring spirits, the girls maintained silence. But after the confession, Abigail Williams, Betty Parris and the other girls admit having associated with the devil. To protect themselves and to shirk an execution, the girls, headed by Abigail, accuse other people of witchcraft. Abigail names, amongst others, Elizabeth Proctor. Abigail hopes that Elizabeth will be executed, assuming that John Proctor, with whom Abigail was engaged in an affair, will marry her. Elizabeth Proctor is arrested and if she does not confess, she will be hanged, just like all the other accused. Although there is no

---

[5] http://www.kennedy-
center.org/calendar/index.cfm?fuseaction=showIndividual&entitY_id=3762&source_type=A
[6] http://www.sparknotes.com/lit/crucible/summary.html

evidence, the two judges Danforth and Hathorne believe in declarations of implausible girls.

John Proctor, in order to save his wife, convinces Mary Warren, his maid and one of the girls in the forest, to tell the truth and to testify that Abigail and the other girls are lying and not possessed by the devil. To do not leak out in the court Abigail pretends that Mary bewitches her. Mary Warren is not preserving, she breaks down and accuses John Proctor to be a witch. He is arrested and executed because he told the truth and did not concede something he had not done.

Abigail Williams runs away, her false accusations were vain, they only caused deaths.

2.3 Character Constellation

The Crucible, unlike other plays of Arthur Miller, has a large number of characters. This number is a sign of the huge number of victims, executed in the play.

Abigail Williams, the niece of Reverend Paris, is a key figure. Her activities are crucial to the development of the drama. Abigail's anger and frustration, based on the dismissal from the Proctor's household, leads to the never-ending accusations.

John Proctor is the central character in the play. He, a victim of charges himself, is situated in a conflict between his personal conscience and the public pressure.

Elizabeth Proctor, the wife of John Proctor, is not a central character in the play. Instead of her person, the love for her husband takes a centre stage.

Judge Danforth, unlike Judge Hathorne, plays a denotative role in the drama. He, the "Deputy Governor of the province Massachusetts"[7], represents the authority of Church and State in the society. Blinded by his religious conviction, Judge Danforth loses the sight of the intrigue, headed by Abigail Williams.

---

[7] Mahoney, John. "Guide to The Crucible", Charles Letts & CO. Ltd: London, 1988, p.67

Reverend Hale and Reverend Parris, the two ministers, are key characters as well. Reverend Hale is the one who is well schooled in witches and who should banish the evil spirits out of Salem.

Reverend Parris, who advises Reverend Hale of the alleged witchcraft, is very self-absorbed. As he thinks that his daughter's illness is based on witchcraft, he loses the overview about what is real and what is simulated.

Betty Parris, Mercy Lewis, Mary Warren and Tituba do not play an important role in the drama. The girls, who attended the dance in the forest, are influenced by Abigail Williams. They only assist Abigail in maintaining the rumours of witchcraft.

Giles Corey and Rebecca Nurse are two of the large number of accused and condemned persons. As they are good friends of John Proctor, they appear several times in the play, actual they stand for the multitude of victims.

2.3.1. Relationship John Proctor – Abigail Williams

Abigail Williams was the housekeeper of John and Elizabeth Proctor. While working in the Proctor's house, she fell in love with John and had an affair with him. The affair constituted a sin according to the puritan way of thinking. On this account John Proctor and Abigail Williams conceal their carry-on from the bourgeoisie, Proctor considering his wife Elizabeth as well.

Abigail, with her unsatisfied sexual needs, holds Elizabeth responsible for Proctor withdrawing from her. John Proctor regrets the affair with Abigail and clarifies that there won't be any affair again.

To take revenge on Elizabeth and to hold the chance to marry John Proctor up, Abigail does not shrink away from accusing Elizabeth of witchcraft.

However, Abigail does not bargain for the confession of John Proctor as to adultery. John Proctor sides with his wife, Abigail frustrated and all set to "kill to gain the man for whom she lusts"[8], charges more and more people. In doing so, she does not notice John Proctor keeping himself distance from her.

2.3.2 Relationship John Proctor – Elizabeth Proctor

After John Proctor committed adultery, the relationship of John and Elizabeth

---

[8] Dukore, Bernard F.. "Death of a Salesman and The Crucible"; Humanities Press International: Atlantic Highlands, 1989. p.52

Proctor is very charged. Although he regrets the affair with Abigail, Elizabeth cannot forgive him and trust him again. The situation escalates when John meets Abigail over again to clarify that the affair was a fault and nothing else. Furthermore, John Proctor forgets the commandment of adultery.

The real love between John and Elizabeth arises at the end of the drama, when Elizabeth comes to John's defence in court and when she accepts his decision rather to die than to confess and base his life on a lie.

2.4 The Role of Religion

Puritanism was a reform movement, emanated from the Church of England, in the 16th and 17th century.

A lot of Puritans emigrated from England to the New England State in the 17th century and this led to Puritanism for the prevalent religion in these states.

2.4.1 The Meaning of Puritanism

The Puritans believed in the tenets of Calvinism, moreover in the predestination.

All humans were sinners, but some of these were justified by Jesus Christ. Puritanism made a point of self-discipline and the Puritans were convinced that God chose them to fight against the disbelief in the church.

In the centre of Puritanism was the conversion of the society, an ideal of bourgeoisie, which equated the commandments.

2.4.2 Consequences of Puritanism in The Crucible

In Arthur Miller's The Crucible there is no difference between the state and the church. Moral laws and the state laws are the same. The people have to decide either to belong to God or to the devil.

In The Crucible Reverend John Hale wants "to put some questions as to the Christian character"[9] of their house, to Elizabeth and John Proctor.

Hale wants to know the circumstances, why they are "rarely in Church on Sabbath Day"[10] and why only two of their three children are baptized.

---

[9] Miller, Arthur. "The Crucible"; Dramatists Play Service: New York, 195, p.36
[10] Miller, Arthur. "The Crucible"; Dramatists Play Service: New York, 195, p.36

By saying the truth, that he does not like "that Mister Parris should lay his hand upon"[11] his baby and that he sees "no light of God in that man"[12], John Proctor makes a suspicion impression on Reverend Hale.

Furthermore Hale is interested whether Elizabeth Proctor knows the Ten Commandments or not. After Elizabeth affirms that she knows the commandments, Reverend Hale demands John Proctor to name them.

Proctor forgets one commandment, adultery, but to forget only one means just a "small fault"[13] to John Proctor.

However Reverend Hale exhorts John Proctor and points at the theology as a fortress and "no crack in a fortress may be accounted small"[14].

In court, while Judge Danforth questions Francis Nurse, the principles of Puritanism are visible.

Judge Danforth makes clear "that a person is either with this court or he must be counted against it; there is no road between"[15]. The people have to decide either to be with the court, which means to be with God, or against court, which means to be with the devil.

Not to take stand to the religion means not to take stand to the state and this is not acquiesced.

---

[11] Miller, Arthur. "The Crucible"; Dramatists Play Service: New York, 195, p.37
[12] Miller, Arthur. "The Crucible"; Dramatists Play Service: New York, 195, p.37
[13] Miller, Arthur. "The Crucible"; Dramatists Play Service: New York, 195, p.38
[14] Miller, Arthur. "The Crucible"; Dramatists Play Service: New York, 195, p.38
[15] Miller, Arthur. "The Crucible"; Dramatists Play Service: New York, 195, p.58

3. Joseph McCarthy

3.1 Biography

Joseph Raymond McCarthy was born on a farm near Appleton, Wisconsin, in 1908.

He had an invariable childhood - he went to elementary education in a "small, one-room country school"[16] and worked on his father's farm. He was a withdrawn child, without connections to "the great world which lay beyond the boundaries of the family farm"[17].

In the summer of 1929, Joseph McCarthy went to Manawa to manage a grocery store. In the same year he entered the Little Wolf High School where he "rushed through the normal high school curriculum in one short year"[18].

In 1930 McCarthy was permitted to attend the Marquette University in Milwaukee. First he studied engineering, but soon switched to law. Shortly after gaining his law degree in 1935, Joseph McCarthy joined a lawyer's office in Shawano.

In 1936 Joseph McCarthy was elected president of the "district's Young Democratic Club"[19] and at the age of 30, he "became the youngest circuit judge ever elected in Wisconsin"[20].

In 1942 McCarthy volunteered for the armed services and he was delegated a "first lieutenant in the Marines"[21]. In 1943 he joined the American forces in the Pacific and "participated in combat bombing missions"[22].

In 1944 Joseph McCarthy decided to run for Wisconsin's Republican senatorial nomination. Therefore he left the Marine Corps in July and came home to campaign. But many Republicans remained suspicious, because in 1936 McCarthy ran as a Democrat and in 1944 as a Republican. In 1944 McCarthy lost the campaign for the U.S. Senate, but in 1946 he stand up to

---

[16] Reeves, Thomas C.. "McCarthyism"; Robert E. Krieger Publishing Company: New York, 1978, p.1
[17] Reeves, Thomas C.. "McCarthyism"; Robert E. Krieger Publishing Company: New York, 1978, p.1
[18] Reeves, Thomas C.. "McCarthyism"; Robert E. Krieger Publishing Company: New York, 1978, p.2
[19] Reeves, Thomas C.. "McCarthyism"; Robert E. Krieger Publishing Company: New York, 1978, p.2
[20] www.apl.org/ HISTORY/mccarthy/biography.html
[21] www.apl.org/ HISTORY/mccarthy/biography.html
[22] www.apl.org/ HISTORY/mccarthy/biography.html

Robert M. LaFollette. He won the campaign and became, with the age of 38, the youngest member of the new Senate.

In 1949 Joseph McCarthy started a "personal witch hunt for communists in the government that lasted for more than five years"[23]. Although a special Senate committee ascertained the charges without finding any evidence for communism and for espionage, McCarthy waged "a relentless anti-communist crusade"[24].

In 1952 McCarthy was re-elected with 59% of the votes. One year later he became president of the Committee Government Operations.

In this time, Joseph McCarthy "seemingly out-of-control"[25] was making many enemies by accusations and investigations against the army.

In December 1954 the Senate "passed a resolution condemning McCarthy for abusing his power as senator"[26].

Joseph Raymond McCarthy died in 1957 of hepatitis in Bethesda, Maryland.

3.2 McCarthyism – Political Situation of the American 1950s

McCarthyism describes a severe anti-communist campaign, in the American 1950s, headed by Senator Joseph McCarthy.

With the end of World War II. in spring 1945, the Cold War began. The Cold War was a period of conflict and tension between the United States and the Sowjet Union. In this time the "anticommunism moved to the ideological center of the American politics."[27] With this attitude the United Stated viewed the Communist party (CPUSA) as potential secret agents of the Sowjet Union. Therefore McCarthyism, which has a more general meaning today and not necessarily referring to the scheme of Joseph McCarthy, started with the Cold War.

The triggering factor of a lasting anti-communist campaign was Joseph McCarthy's Wheeling speech on Lincoln Day, February 9th in 1950, in Wheeling, West Virginia.

---

[23] http://www.cnn.com/SPECIALS/cold.war/kbank/profiles/mccarthy/
[24] http://us.history.wisc.edu/hist102/bios/31.html
[25] http://www.cnn.com/SPECIALS/cold.war/kbank/profiles/mccarthy/
[26] http://www.freeinfosociety.com/site.php?postnum=78
[27] http://www.writing.upenn.edu/~afilreis/50s/menace-emerges.html

In this speech McCarthy pretended that a communist revolution won't be carried out peacefully and he called on the audience not to be blind, but to notice the engagement of the United States in the "final, all-out battle between communist atheism and Christianity"[28]. Furthermore, McCarthy published a list of 205 names "that were made known to the Secretary of State as being members of the Communist Party and who nevertheless are still working and shaping policy in the State Department"[29]. In the end of his speech, Joseph McCarthy proclaimed the persons on his list as being guilty of high treason to the United States.

The speech resulted in a keen interest of the press in McCarthy, which entailed his activities getting into focus.

In order to investigate communist activities, the House Un-American Activities Committee (HUAC), the Senate Internal Security Subcommittee and the Senate Permanent Subcommittee on Investigations were the most important institutions during McCarthyism. From 1949 till 1954, 109 investigations were made by these committees.

Another offence of Joseph McCarthy and the committees commenced in 1950 with the publishing of the "Red Channels: The Report of Communists in Radio and Television"[30]. The blacklist named 151 names of actors, writers, musicians, broadcast journalists and other people of the entertainment industry who were suspected to be communists.

3.3 Accusations and victims

A number of victims of the Era of McCarthyism is difficult to diagnose. The victims were not only accused and imprisoned, but in the majority of cases an accusation sufficed to lose ones job. People who were mentioned in the blacklist or were charged by one of the committees had no chance to find a new employment.

---

[28] Wheeling Speech; http://www.u-cergy.fr/brobert/McCarthy_Wheeling_Speech.pdf
[29] Wheeling Speech; http://www.u-cergy.fr/brobert/McCarthy_Wheeling_Speech.pdf
[30] http://www.authentichistory.com/1950s/redchannels/redchannels.html

More than hundred people are said to be imprisoned and several thousands lost their jobs. The accused people had no rights, they were neither authorised to hear the name of the accuser nor the causes.

Some famous personages who were accused in the McCarthy-Era were Aaron Copland (composer), Orson Welles (actor, author and director), Robert Oppenheimer (physicist), Leonard Bernstein (composer), Charlie Chaplin (actor), Bertold Brecht (poet) and Arthur Miller (author).

3.4 The decline of McCarthyism

The downfall of Joseph McCarthy started in 1953, when McCarthy, obsessed with anti-communist thoughts, accused the United States Army of protecting suspected communists. A committee researched the reproaches against the Army in the Army-McCarthy hearings, which started on April 22nd 1954 and lasted 36 days. The hearings were crucial to the end of Senator Joseph McCarthy, as it was the first hearing published in television. Some of the television networks attending the hearings, "covered every moment, totalling more than 188 hours"[31].

The audience was a voucher of an intensive hearing, which was "a marathon of accusation"[32] and which was conducted by Joseph McCarthy and his counsel on the one side and by Joseph Welch, the attorney of the United States Army, on the other side.

Joseph McCarthy shocked the audience and the people who were watching the hearings on television; he was "abusive, threatening, defiant and disorderly"[33]. Additional McCarthy denunciated everyone, the president, the Army, the State Department and nearly "every one of the senators who was sitting in judgement upon him"[34].

On June 9th, the 30th day of the Army-McCarthy-hearings, the trial hit his peak. Joseph McCarthy accused, out of the blue, Fred Fisher, a lawyer working in Joseph Welch's Boston law office. Fred Fisher had once belonged

---

[31] http://mattstodayinhistory.blogspot.com/2007/04/army-mccarthy-hearings-april-22-1954_22.html
[32] Latham, Earl. "The Meaning of McCarthyism"; Second Edition; D.C. Heath and Company: Lexington, Massachusetts, 1973, p.191
[33] Latham, Earl. "The Meaning of McCarthyism"; Second Edition; D.C. Heath and Company: Lexington, Massachusetts, 1973, p.191
[34] Latham, Earl. "The Meaning of McCarthyism"; Second Edition; D.C. Heath and Company: Lexington, Massachusetts, 1973, p.191

to the National Lawyers Guilt; however this was no evidence of a connection to communism. Welch, with a lack of understanding for McCarthy's accusations made up out if thin air, defended Fred Fisher with a "monologue nearly six minutes long"[35], and ending in the lines:

"Until this moment, senator, I think I never gauged your cruelty or recklessness....Have you no sense of decency, sir, at long last? Have you left no sense of decency?"[36]

A few weeks later, on June 17th, the Army-McCarthy-hearings ended. There were no convictions, neither against the Army, nor civilians. In December 1954 the Senate pronounced their mistrust against McCarthy and his anti-communist campaign. Afterwards Joseph McCarthy was censured.

---

[35] http://mattstodayinhistory.blogspot.com/2007/04/army-mccarthy-hearings-april-22-1954_22.html
[36] http://mattstodayinhistory.blogspot.com/2007/04/army-mccarthy-hearings-april-22-1954_22.html

4. Relation between <u>The Crucible</u> and McCarthyism

The first relation between the drama <u>The Crucible</u> and the Era of McCarthyism is based on the biography of Arthur Miller. Miller himself was accused of belonging to the communist party and of knowing other communists. Furthermore, Miller was demanded to mention names of communist. He refused to mention random names; therefore he was imprisoned till the end of the Era of McCarthyism.

This situation Arthur Miller was in occurs in the play, when Reverend Hale asks Abigail Williams for names of girls who conjured evil spirits and communicated with the devil. In contrary to Arthur Miller, Abigail and Betty name arbitrary names of girls, later Abigail mentions even more people.

The second parallel is the accusation without any evidence. Joseph McCarthy's blacklist and the Red Channels were baseless. The mention of names sufficed to bring these people to court. The last accusation of Joseph McCarthy during the hearings was an excellent example of the disposal used to find assumed communists. When the people were charged, they were already guilty.

In the drama <u>The Crucible</u>, Abigail Williams has no evidence to proof only one of her statements. Everyday she accused more people of being witches. After John Proctor clarified the end of their affair she charges Elizabeth Proctor, later on she accuses John Proctor because he does not stick with her. The number of accusations and who was accused did not base on evidence, but on the mood of people, in this case of Abigail Williams. Nevertheless, all obvious random charges were investigated by the judge and moreover, the judge believes in what the girls said.

For the accused, either in the Era of McCarthyism or in the drama <u>The Crucible</u>, it is rather impossible to proof their innocence, because nobody can demonstrate something which did not happen, not to mention something they did not do.

The next indication which shows the relation between McCarthyism and <u>The Crucible</u> is the time when the play was written and the time of the anti-communist campaign in the United States. McCarthyism happened in the early 1950s, The Crucible was written in 1953. Other authors, who used the Salem Witch Trials of 1692 as basis of their novels, were Henry Longfellow (Giles Corey of the Salem Farm, 1868), Nathaniel Hawthorne (Young Goodman Brown) and Mary Freeman (Giles Corey, Yeoman, 1893). If Arthur Miller wanted the recollection of the Salem Witch Trials to be the ambition of his drama, he could have written it at another time, just like the other authors mentioned. The fact that he wrote it during McCarthyism shows that the political situation reminded him of the Salem Witch Trials, which are described in The Crucible.

The last obvious parallel between the drama and McCarthyism is the unpunished disappearance of the culprit.

Joseph McCarthy accused people without cause; he destroyed their future by calling them communists, even though he had no evidence. But Joseph McCarthy was not judged and not condemned; he was only relegated out of the Senate. Moreover, his victims had no safe future, but they were dependent on the employers offering a job.

In the play Abigail Williams disappeared in the end with the money of her uncle Reverend Parris. She left nothing, neither a message, nor a declaration which announces the innocence of the accused. Abigail was not judged, but the charged people are hanged although nobody is guilty.

5. Conclusion

In my opinion the relation between the drama The Crucible and McCarthyism is visible by the knowledge of Arthur Miller's background and by the identical behaviour of the protagonists Joseph McCarthy and Abigail Williams.

Furthermore, with regard to the obvious disposals, the accusations and therewith the causeless choice of victims are presented both in the play and in the political situation of the American 1950s.

To my mind the fact that Arthur Miller learned the injustice and the horror of such an intrigue, as McCarthyism was, the hard way, led to the writing of The Crucible and was crucial to it. Miller had to choose another historical event to express the cruelty of the McCarthy-Era, otherwise he would have been accused a second time because of an uprising against the Senate.

The decline of McCarthyism and the leaving of Abigail Williams, in the end of The Crucible, were symbols of the culprits' running off. The escape of Abigail is not fixed on the progression of the Salem Witch Trials in 1692. In my opinion Miller chose this ending as a felicitous fragment of a rightly extolled drama.

I experienced The Crucible as an imposing and absorbing play which reflects historical events and which is conferrable to our time. The Crucible conveys the awareness of danger of scheming which can appear at all times.

6. Bibliography

Miller, Arthur. "The Crucible"; Dramatists Play Service: New York, 1954

Martine, James J.. "Critical Essays on Arthur Miller"; Ed. Martin, Robert A., "The Crucible: Background and Sources"; G.K. Hall & CO.: Boston, Massachusetts, 1979. 93-104

Corrigan, Robert W.. "Arthur Miller A Collection of Critical Essays"; Ed. Warshow, Robert, "The Liberal Conscience in The Crucible"; Prentice-Hall: New Jersey, 1969. 111-121

Dukore, Bernard F.. "Death of a Salesman and The Crucible"; Humanities Press International: Atlantic Highlands, 1989. 41-63

Mahoney, John. "Guide to The Crucible", Charles Letts & CO. Ltd: London, 1988

Reeves, Thomas C.. "McCarthyism"; Robert E. Krieger Publishing Company: New York, 1978

Latham, Earl. "The Meaning of McCarthyism"; Second Edition; D.C. Heath and Company: Lexington, Massachusetts, 1973

May, Ronald, Jack Anderson. "McCarthy"; Trans. Stuebs, Albin; Akros Verlag GmbH: Hamburg, 1953

http://library.thinkquest.org/27864/data/miller/ambio.htm , last access 31/04/08

http://www.kennedy-center.org/calendar/index.cfm?fuseaction=showIndividual&entitY_id=3762&source_type=A, last access 31/04/08 http://www.neh.gov/whoweare/miller/biography.html, last access 31/04/08

http://www.sparknotes.com/lit/crucible/summary.html, last access 31/04/08

http://www.apl.org/ HISTORY/mccarthy/biography.html, last access 07/05/08

http://www.spartacus.schoolnet.co.uk/USAmccarthy.htm, last access 07/05/08

http://academic.brooklyn.cuny.edu/english/melani/novel_18c/defoe/puritanism.html, last access 07/05/08

http://de.encarta.msn.com/encyclopedia_761565242/Puritanismus.html, last access 02/05/08

http://www.sparknotes.com/lit/crucible/themes.html, last access 02/05/08

http://www.cnn.com/SPECIALS/cold.war/kbank/profiles/mccarthy/, last access 06/05/08

http://us.history.wisc.edu/hist102/bios/31.html, last access 06/05/08

http://www.freeinfosociety.com/site.php?postnum=78, last access 06/05/08

http://www.writing.upenn.edu/~afilreis/50s/menace-emerges.html, last access 06/05/08

Wheeling Speech; http://www.u-cergy.fr/brobert/McCarthy_Wheeling_Speech.pdf , last access 06/05/08

http://en.wikipedia.org/wiki/McCarthyism, last access 07/05/08

http://www.authentichistory.com/1950s/redchannels/redchannels.html, last access 06/05/08

http://www.multied.com/postwar/McCarthy.html, last access 07/05/08 http://www.heise.de/tp/r4/artikel/21/21155/1.html, last access 07/05/08

http://mattstodayinhistory.blogspot.com/2007/04/army-mccarthy-hearings-
april-22-1954_22.html, last access 07/05/08

http://www.wsu.edu/~campbelld/amlit/witch.htm#fiction, last access 07/05/08